CONTENTS

INTRODUCTION

If you have ever wanted to know what it feels like to drive some of the most exciting cars in the world then The Need for Speed will show you.

It wasn't long after the automobile was invented that drivers started to race their cars and motor racing was born. It has evolved today into many branches, including stock car racing – drivers in production models modified for the race track.

Stock car racing originated in the United States where it is now one of the most popular spectator sports. Since the 1940s the sport has spread around the world and is now popular in the UK, Europe and Australia.

"Stock car racing" is an umbrella term – at the top of the sport there are races organized by the National Association of Stock Car Auto Racing (NASCAR), stock car racing's governing body in the USA. Here, drivers take the wheels of cars that cost thousands of dollars to develop and maintain. At the other end of the sport there's banger or road hog racing, where weekend enthusiasts crash their way around local tracks in cars one step away from the scrapheap.

NASCAR racing concentrates on speed, and it's on this branch of the sport that we have decided to focus in this book. NASCAR drivers are household names in the USA. Their cars have many things in common, but the most important is The Need for Speed.

As well as giving you a taste of the thrills of NASCAR racing, we also give you the facts and figures behind some of these incredible machines and the tracks where they race. These are found in the Stat Files and Track Files, which look like this.

STAT FILE

LUMINA

Wheelbase	279.5 cm (110 in)
Weight	1586 kg (3500 lb)
Brakes	Ventilated disc brakes
Engine	5867 cc (358 ci), ohv.1-4V, V8, 700 hp
Transmission	Borg Warner Super T-10, floor-shift, four-speed manual

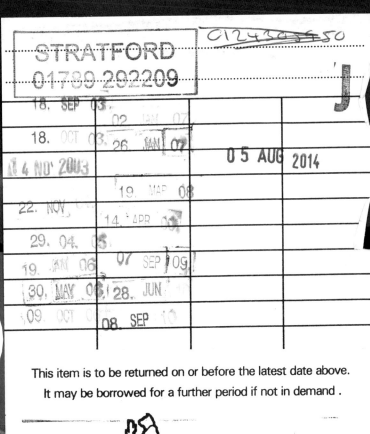

Mike Johnstone

CREDITS

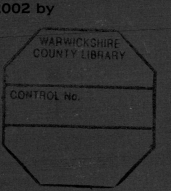

This edition published in 2002 by
Franklin Watts
96 Leonard Street
London EC2A 4XD

Franklin Watts Australia
45-51 Huntley Street
Alexandria
NSW 2015

© Franklin Watts 2001

Designed by: Jason Billin / Billin Design Solutions
Art director: Jonathan Hair
Editor in Chief: John C. Miles

A CIP catalogue record for this book
is available from the British Library

ISBN 0 7496 4754 X

Dewey Decimal Classification 796.7

Printed in Dubai

*Picture credits: All photographs, including details,
supplied by Allsport UK Ltd.*
*Front cover: top (Jamie Squire), middle (Yukio Yoshimi),
bottom (Craig Jones) Back cover: (Yukio Yoshimi) pp. 1 main
(Craig Jones), 1 inset (Yukio Yoshimi), 2-3 main (David
Taylor), 5 main (Jamie Squire), 5 inset (Craig Jones), 6 centre
left (Jamie Squire), 7 main (Robert Laberge), 8 bottom left
and right (Robert Laberge), 9 main (David Taylor), 10 bottom
left (Jon Ferrey), 10-11 centre (Yukio Yoshimi), 11 main
(David Taylor), 11 inset (David Taylor), 12 bottom left (Jamie
Squire) 13 main (Jamie Squire) 13 inset (Chris Stanford), 14
inset (Robert Laberge), 14-15 main (Jamie Squire), 16 centre
(Jonathan Ferrey), 16-17 main (David Taylor), 18 bottom
right (David Taylor), 19 main (Robert Laberge), 20 bottom
(Jamie Squire), 21 main (Jamie Squire), 21 top right (Robert
Laberge), 23 main (Jamie Squire), 23 inset (Jon Ferrey),
24 bottom left (David Taylor), 25 main (Jamie Squire),
25 inset (Robert Laberge), 26 bottom left (Robert Laberge),
27 main (David Taylor), 28 bottom left (David Taylor),
29 main (David Taylor)*

NASCAR

This organization was founded in 1947 by Bill France, one of the pioneers of the sport, who decided that it needed "a little organization". NASCAR sanctioned its first race at Daytona Beach the following year and has overseen the sport in the USA ever since.

It is NASCAR who decides the modifications that may be made to a car while still retaining its "stock" status within its class, one of its aims being that all cars raced in that class are as equal as possible.

The Fact File gives you a slightly unusual, strange or funny bit of information.

FACT FILE

Leading stock car drivers have to be very fit to cope with the physical demands of driving their cars at such high speeds for long periods. Drivers work out in the gym every day and many cycle long distances on mountain bikes to keep fit.

In November 1895, J Frank Duryea, driving a car he had made himself, won a race that started in Chicago, Illinois, and finished in Evanston, 84 km (52.4 miles) away. He took ten hours to complete the course! As cars grew in popularity, mechanics started tinkering with them to make them go faster, and in 1909 the first race to be billed "stock car" was run over 37 km (23 miles) of Long Island, USA, streets.

In 1915, a stock car race was run on a specially built wooden track at the Chicago Speedway. But it was a few years later, at a beach in Florida, that stock car racing really took off after car manufacturers decided to hold timed trials there.

The competitive spirit soon took over and within a few months races were being run along the beach and the adjoining road. The beach was at Daytona – still regarded by stock car enthusiasts as the birthplace of their sport.

In Europe, at the same time, impromptu races were being held wherever there were drivers and a suitable area in which to create some sort of track. But it was not until the 1950s that organized stock car racing began in Europe. It was brought to Britain after a successful series of races had been held at the Buffalo Stadium in Paris in 1953-4. The sport in the UK is now divided into two classes - Formula 1 and Formula 2 - each with its own rules and competitions. It is growing in popularity all the time, as in Australia where organized Hot Rod Racing has been part of the sporting calendar for more than 40 years.

Why all the adverts?

Professional stock car racing is very expensive, and racing teams depend on big companies to give them money. In return, the teams put sponsors' logos all over their cars so everyone at the track and watching on TV can see them. It's a highly visible form of advertising.

FACT FILE

Race day

NASCAR races are held on oval-shaped tracks. The corners slope inwards so that the cars can go around them at speeds nearing 322 km/h (200 mph). The cars always race in an anticlockwise direction. The cars need to be very tough, as in NASCAR it is acceptable for vehicles to collide. At the end of the race many cars are badly dented. Some don't finish the race.

DOING THE ROUNDS

There is a huge variety of race tracks holding NASCAR events all over the USA. But many tracks hold non-NASCAR races as well.

Among the most professional circuits there are tracks such as Bristol Motor Speedway in Tennessee, nicknamed "The World's Fastest Half-Mile", with its track banked to 36 degrees to keep the cars from flying off. Two states north, in Indiana, there's Brownstown Speedway, half the length of Bristol and banked to just ten degrees. Brownstown is a great favourite with fans of Dirt Late Model racing. This sport became hugely popular in the 1990s, when it was heavily featured on cable and satellite television.

Some tracks have huge grandstands and lavish hospitality suites where wealthy sponsors entertain their guests in style. On the other hand, there is Road Hog racing, where old Lincolns, Fords and Chevvies bang bumpers and spin off the track as their amateur drivers put them through their paces. Spectators here may be offered little more than a wooden seat on a grassy bank, with a hot dog stand nearby. Either way it's a great day (or night) out.

For NASCAR events, thousands of fans cram the trackside stands to watch Jeff Gordon and other star drivers pit their skills against one another in lap after thrilling lap.

Pre-race parades give little hint of the thrills in store for spectators.

Each circuit has trackside pits where drivers refuel their cars.

FACT FILE

The Winston Cup

The Winston Cup is the top prize for all top stock car drivers. Sponsored by one of the world's largest tobacco companies, the Cup is competed for in a series of races run over more than 20 tracks throughout the USA.

NASCAR lays down strict rules to ensure that all Winston Cup contenders' cars are as equal as possible. For example, drivers who weigh in at less than 72 kg (160 lbs) must add lead weights to their cars so that they gain no advantage from their trim figures!

FACT FILE

The Busch Grand National Series

The BGN is sometimes called the Winston Cup's little brother. BGN cars are powered by the same V8 engines as their bigger relatives, but are not as highly tuned.

Busch cars have a 267 cm (105 in) wheelbase, 12.7 cm (5 in) less than Winston competitors. This makes a huge difference in handling. Most of the stars of the Winston Cup, including Jeff Gordon, honed their race skills in the BGN series.

CHEVROLET

Chevrolet is one of the big names in NASCAR. A glance at the Winston Cup Roll of Honor shows that since 1957 Chevy drivers have won the biggest prize of stock car racing 20 times, including six years in succession from 1993 to 1998.

In 1955 Chevrolet unveiled their 4343 cubic-centimetre (265 cubic-inch) small-block V8 engine. It consigned nearly every other engine design to the scrapheap.

No other engine at the time could develop 180 hp at 4800 rpm with an 8:1 compression ratio and a four-barrel carburettor. Two years later, a car powered by an improved version reached 209 km/h (130 mph) at Daytona Beach.

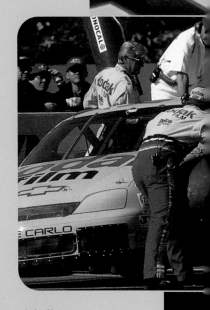

Chevrolet sat on the sidelines in the 1960s, but they came back in the 70s when Cale Yarborough left Ford and took the wheel of a Chevrolet Laguna S-3 which he took to the 246 km/h (153 mph) mark at Darlington, South Carolina. The late, great Dale Earnhardt's 1979-80 Chevy Monte Carlo and Ernie Irvan's 1991 Lumina were worthy successors.

The 1990s saw the Chevrolet-driving trio of Dale Earnhardt, Terry Labonte and Jeff Gordon winning again and again. The current Lumina is one of the fastest cars on the Winston Cup circuit with a possible top speed in excess of 322 km/h (200 mph).

STAT FILE

LUMINA

Wheelbase	279.5 cm (110 in)
Weight	1586 kg (3500 lb)
Brakes	Ventilated disc brakes
Engine	5867 cc (358 ci), ohv.1-4V, V8, 700 hp
Transmission	Borg Warner Super T-10, floor-shift, four-speed manual

DAYTONA

Whoever it was who had the idea to hold timed trials at Daytona Beach in Florida can have had little idea of what they were starting. Today, Daytona is the most famous stock car race track in the world; indeed to many people Daytona is stock car racing!

As cars increased their speed in the 1930s, timed trials moved from Daytona to the safer salt flats of Bonneville in Utah, but stock car drivers decided that it was still acceptable to carry on racing at Daytona. Their decision was backed by the American Automobile Association who sanctioned a race there in 1936.

The race was won by Louis Meyer at the wheel of a 1934 Ford. He somehow managed to steer his car at high speed through the deep ruts that developed on the turns.

As more and more ruts formed in later races, drivers started to slide their cars around the bends with spectacular results: some cars flipped over, others lost springs, oil pans and other parts.

More and more drivers headed for the beach at Daytona and, attracted by the prospect of thrills and spills, crowds of spectators followed.

FACT FILE

The Victory Lane

When Winston Cup races are over, the victors take their places in Daytona's Victory Lane. The list of drivers who have brought their cars to a halt here is a roll call of some of the United States' best-known stock car racers.

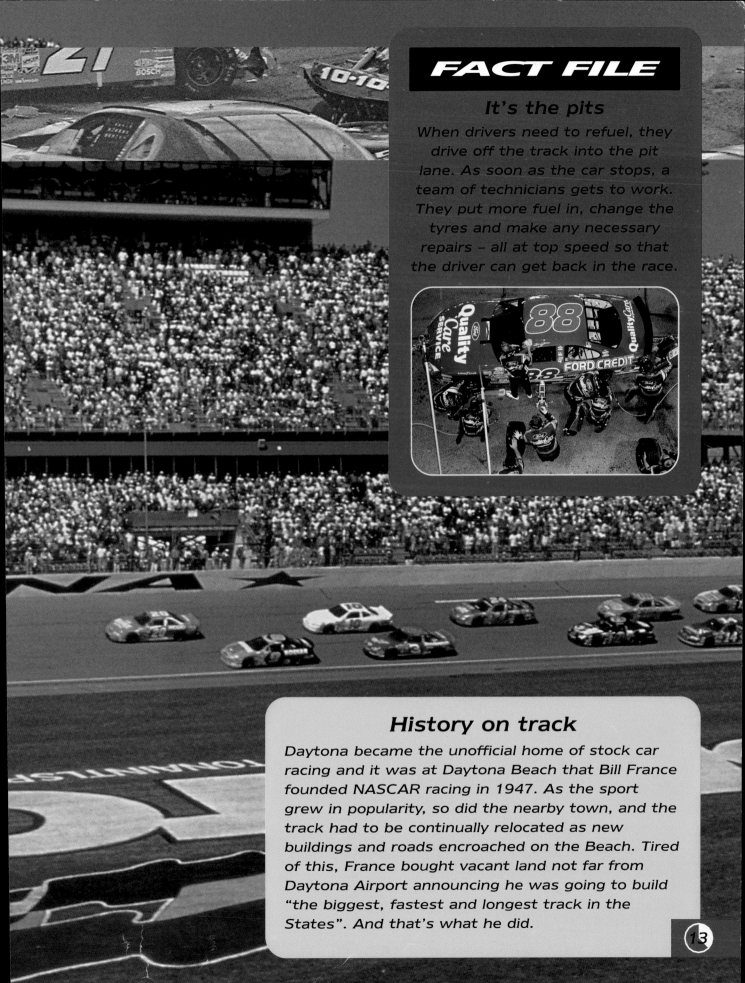

It's the pits

When drivers need to refuel, they drive off the track into the pit lane. As soon as the car stops, a team of technicians gets to work. They put more fuel in, change the tyres and make any necessary repairs – all at top speed so that the driver can get back in the race.

History on track

Daytona became the unofficial home of stock car racing and it was at Daytona Beach that Bill France founded NASCAR racing in 1947. As the sport grew in popularity, so did the nearby town, and the track had to be continually relocated as new buildings and roads encroached on the Beach. Tired of this, France bought vacant land not far from Daytona Airport announcing he was going to build "the biggest, fastest and longest track in the States". And that's what he did.

DAYTONA INTERNATIONAL SPEEDWAY

Every February, more than 165,000 fans cram the stands at Daytona to watch the Daytona 500, the inaugural race in the NASCAR calendar. It is the culmination of Daytona's "February Speedweek" – seven days of racing including the all-star "Bud Shoot-Out" for Winston Cup pole position winners of the previous year.

Later on in the year, at the beginning of July, the floodlit Pepsi 400 attracts capacity crowds. The race is one of the hottest in the Winston Cup calendar; literally one of the hottest, for the Florida heat can send the temperature on track soaring to 52° C (125° F).

It was at Daytona, in 1976, that Richard Petty lost one of the most memorable races in Winston Cup history. Petty and his close rival David Pearson were neck and neck coming into the last lap. After touching a few times, they crashed hard and spun off the track. Somehow Pearson managed to keep his car running, got it back on track and nursed it across the finishing line to win!

The new complex, Daytona USA, which opened in July 1996, is more than a race track: it's a 194 hectare (480 acre) multi-million dollar motorsports mecca with something for everyone in the least bit interested in motor racing.

Hold that power

Concerned that companies sponsoring Winston Cup teams encourage their drivers to bunch together at dangerously high speed during televised races at Daytona (and Talladega in Alabama), NASCAR insist that cars at these tracks are fitted with carburettor restrictor plates that limit horsepower and therefore reduce speed.

STAT FILE

Daytona Trackfacts

Length	4 km (2.5 miles)
Width	12.2 m (40 ft)
Banking	31 degrees on the turns, 18 degrees on the trioval
Total frontstretch	1158 m (3800 ft)
Pit road	488 m (1600 ft) long, 15.2 m (50 ft) wide

FACT FILE

Qualifying Records	Driver	Speed	Date
NASCAR WINSTON CUP	B. Elliot	338.548 km/h (210.364 mph)	9.2.87
BUSCH GRAND NATIONAL	T. Houston	312.839 km/h (194.389 mph)	10.2.87
Race Records	Driver	Speed	Date
NASCAR WINSTON CUP	B. Allison	279.178 km/h (173.473 mph)	4.7.80
BUSCH GRAND NATIONAL	G. Bodine	252.887 km/h (157.137 mph)	16.2.85

For most stock car racing enthusiasts around the world, the nearest track is a short distance away.

In the USA there are stock car race tracks all over the country from east coast to west, from towns on the Mexican border in the south to cities on the northern border with Canada. It's only possible to list a few in the pages of this book: here's some information on four of the best.

ATLANTA MOTOR SPEEDWAY

First built in 1960 and modernized in the 1990s, Atlanta Motor Speedway at Hampton, Georgia is very popular with fans of stock car racing. The original 2.449 km (1.522 mile) oval track was relaid and extended to 2.479 km (1.54 miles). The banking is 24 degrees, making it a steep challenge for even the best drivers, among them Geoff Bodine who lapped the track in 28.074 seconds, reaching 317.810 km/h (197.478 mph) and Bobby Labonte who averaged a record 273.434 km/h (169.904 mph) during the same Winston Cup 800 km (500 mile) race in November 1997.

MICHIGAN SPEEDWAY

The designers of Daytona International Speedway were also the brains behind the track at Brooklyn in Michigan. Almost every seat in the grandstand affords a view of the entire 3.2 km (2 mile) track with its 18 degree banking on the turns.

The track is wide enough for three, sometimes four cars to be racing side-by-side at speeds approaching 322 km/h (200 mph). Dale Jarrett set the race record of 280.013 km/h (173.997 mph) on 13.6.99; Dale Earnhardt Jr holds the qualifying record with a speed of 301.616 km/h (191.149 mph) on 18.8.00.

RICHMOND INTERNATIONAL RACEWAY

Stock car racing has been held at Richmond, Virginia since the 1940s, first on a 0.805 km (0.5 mile) long dirt track. This was paved in 1968. Twenty years later, the track was extended to 1.2 km (0.75 miles) and relaid in a D-shape.

Richmond is one of the most modern tracks on the Winston Cup circuit. Many races are held at night under lights. Jeff Gordon lapped Richmond in 21.344 seconds averaging 203.804 km/h (126.499 mph) in May 1997, which is still a record. And no one has managed to beat Dale Jarrett's 174.936 km/h (108.70 mph) race average which he achieved here in September 1997.

LOWE'S MOTOR SPEEDWAY

The track at Concord in North Carolina is one of the largest outdoor sport stadiums in the southeastern USA, seating 167,000 fans. It hosts three Winston Cup races each year including the Coca-Cola 600 held on Memorial Day. Lowe's owners were among the first to mount pre-race entertainments such as car, motorbike and bus jumps. They were also the first to install floodlights and stage night racing.

The track is 2.4 km (1.5 miles) long with 24 degree banking. Dale Earnhardt Jr reached 299.343 km/h (186.034 mph) when he set the lap record of 29.027 seconds in May 2000. Jeff Gordon's average speed of 257.980 km/h (160.306 mph) set in October 1999, still stands as the record.

General Motors' Pontiac cars had their first NASCAR win in 1957. In 1962, Glenn "Fireball" Roberts and his fellow Pontiac drivers won 22 of that season's 55 Winston Cup races. Pontiac withdrew factory backing in 1963, and although Pontiacs were still seen at minor-league tracks all over the States, they were out of the running in the Winston.

In 1981, however, Pontiac decided to come back to the NASCAR starting grid. Since then drivers such as the legendary Richard Petty and Rusty Wallace have driven Pontiacs to victory in race after race, and it was in a Pontiac Grand Prix that Wallace won the Winston in 1989.

The current Pontiac Grand Prix was introduced in 1996, four years after Petty finished his record-breaking 200-victory career. It is rounder and smoother than the long-nose models that marked Pontiac's return to the race track in the 1980s. It's a sleek aerodynamic wonder, slipping through the wind like a hot knife through butter. The body is built of flat sheet metal stretched over fully fabricated tubular steel frames. Under the bonnet there's an assortment of General Motors components.

The engine, built around a Chevrolet small-block, can produce 700 hp which is enough to propel a race-tuned Grand Prix to over 322 km/h (200 mph). Chevrolet parts are used for the front suspension and a Ford 22.9 cm (9 in) differential is mounted at the rear.

Screw-jack adjustable coil springs and four gas-charged shock absorbers are mounted, one on each wheel, to give the driver a smooth ride.

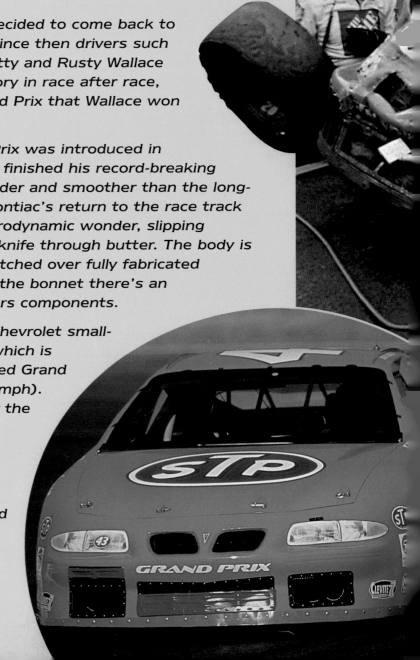

STAT FILE

PONTIAC GRAND PRIX

Wheelbase	279.4 cm (110 in)
Weight	1542 kg (3400 lb)
Brakes	Ventilated disc brakes
Engine	5867 cc (358 ci), ohv.1-4V, V8, 700 hp
Transmission	Borg Warner Super T-10, floor-shift, four-speed manual

MARTINSVILLE

Halfway between Roanoke in Virginia and Greensboro in North Carolina sits the only track from NASCAR's first year still to hold regular stock car races.

Martinsville was opened in 1947 and laid as a dirt track in 1955. The circuit was paved in 1995 and now sits at the centre of a racing complex that covers 121 hectares (300 acres). It attracts race fans and competitors from all over the USA.

For days before each meeting, transporter trucks with cars chained securely to their backs cram the roads leading to the track. Before the racing starts, the drivers are introduced to the cheering fans in a splendidly organized pre-match ceremony with all the razzmatazz one expects from a major US sporting event.

At 0.847 km (0.526 miles) long, Martinsville is the shortest track on the NASCAR circuit. However, all the top drivers rate it as one of the best. The banking may not be the steepest and the straights aren't long enough to really put your foot down and reach top speed, but no driver completes 500 laps at Martinsville without being thoroughly tested.

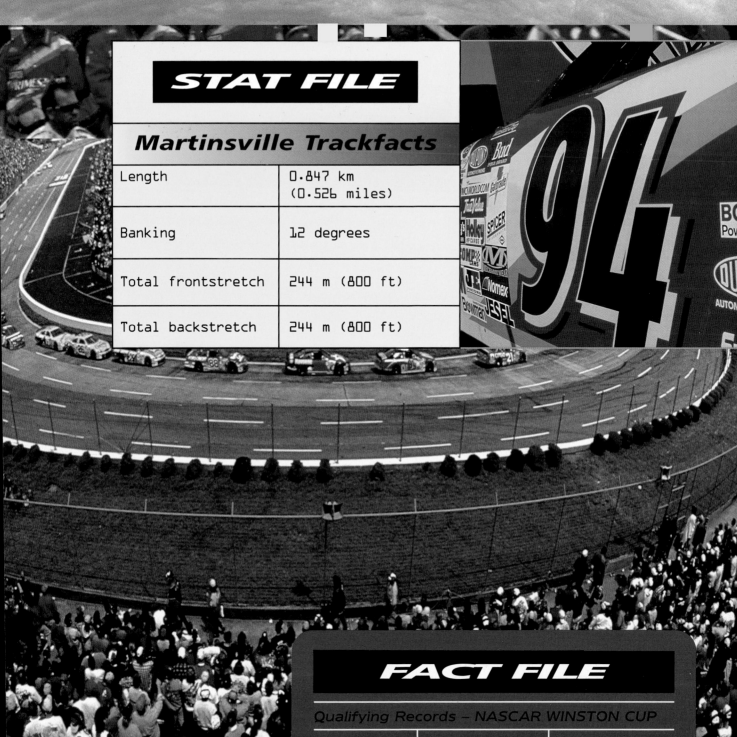

Martinsville Trackfacts

Length	0.847 km (0.526 miles)
Banking	12 degrees
Total frontstretch	244 m (800 ft)
Total backstretch	244 m (800 ft)

FACT FILE

Qualifying Records – NASCAR WINSTON CUP		
Driver	Speed	Date
T. Stewart	153.485 km/h (95.371 mph)	29.9.00
Race Records – NASCAR WINSTON CUP		
Driver	Speed	Date
J. Gordon	132.325 km/h (82.223 mph)	22.8.96

BRISTOL

When Tennessee's Bristol Motor Speedway first opened in 1961, the track was 0.8047 km (exactly 0.5 mile) long. Drivers quickly made it one of the speediest tracks on the NASCAR circuit, earning it the nickname "The World's Fastest Half Mile".

At the opening race, 30,000 enthusiasts cheered Johnny Allen as he crossed the finishing line first, but his name doesn't feature in the record books as he was the relief driver for Jack Smith who got the credit for winning Bristol's inaugural race.

Track and spectator facilities have been upgraded over the past 40 years. In 1992, the track was repaved with concrete. There's now seating for 135,000 fans, the track has been extended slightly and the original 22 degree banking increased by 14 degrees. This makes for some exciting moments when drivers of the calibre of Rusty Wallace take a bend at top speed with rivals hot on his tail.

Before a race at Bristol or any other NASCAR track, teams of technicians are hard at work under the bonnet doing whatever they can to ensure that when the cars line up for the start they are race-tuned to perfection.

FACT FILE

Qualifying Records	Driver	Speed	Time	Date
NASCAR WINSTON CUP	S. Park	203.373 km/h (126.370 mph)	15.184 secs	24.3.00
BUSCH GRAND NATIONAL	J. Green	200.247 km/h (124.428 mph)	15.421 secs	24.3.00
Race records	Driver	Speed	Date	
WINSTON CUP	C. Glotzbach	162.663 km/h (101.074 mph)	11.7.71	
BUSCH	H. Gant	149.555 km/h (92.929 mph)	4.4.92	

STAT FILE

BRISTOL TRACKFACTS

Length	Banking
0.857 km (0.533 miles)	36 degrees

As the clock ticks away and the start gets nearer, teams make last-minute checks to ensure that the cars are in peak condition for the race to come.

In the USA, top stock car drivers are celebrities with their own web sites and fan clubs. Drivers such as Jeff Gordon and Bobby Labonte are household names.

Richard Petty, the all-time great Winston Cup race winner who drove the victor's lane 200 times before he retired in 1992, is a name known to millions of Americans coast to coast. His son, Kyle, and late grandson, Adam, also took to the driver's seat. The Petty name is destined to be remembered for years to come.

As top NASCAR drivers, the Pettys know that even though their names become well known, they are still part of a team. It's no good being the best driver in the world if your car is going to break down at the first bend.

FACT FILE

Top class stock car drivers have to be very fit to cope with the physical demands of driving their cars at such high speeds for long periods. Drivers work out in the gym every day and many cycle long distances on mountain bikes to keep fit.

They also need experience. It helps if racing is a family tradition, but all the great drivers have learned their craft in the lower ranks of stock car racing before hitting the Winston Cup trail. Starting young is a great advantage. Jeff Gordon, for instance, was putting racing sprint cars through their paces when he was 13.

Davey Allison, whose career was cut short when he was killed in a helicopter crash in 1993, was even younger when he started his racing career. He began by tinkering with engines at the family's race shop when he was just 12!

A sad loss

Dale Earnhardt, too, was a youngster when he took the wheel in the early 1970s. He went on to win 76 NASCAR races and seven Winston Cups. His career came to a tragic end at the Daytona 500 in 2001. Coming into the last bend of the last lap his car hit a wall and he was killed instantly. Lying third, he is thought to have been trying to prevent cars behind passing the driver lying second – his son, Dale Jnr.

Dale Earnhardt's famous number 3.

NASCAR WINSTON CUP CHAMPIONS 1991-2000

1991	Dale Earnhardt, Chevy
1992	Alan Kulwicki, Ford
1993	Dale Earnhardt, Chevy
1994	Dale Earnhardt, Chevy
1995	Jeff Gordon, Chevy
1996	Terry Labonte, Chevy
1997	Jeff Gordon, Chevy
1998	Jeff Gordon, Chevy
1999	Dale Jarrett, Ford
2000	Bobby Labonte, Pontiac

INDIANAPOLIS

The track at Indianapolis, Indiana, is best known as the home of the famous Indy 500, "the world's greatest race" first run in 1911. NASCAR ran its first Winston Cup series event here in 1994 and it has been a firm favourite ever since.

Shortly after the track opened in 1909, the original crushed stone and tar track surface started to crack. It was repaved with over 3.2 million bricks and has been known as "The Brickyard" ever since. One strip of the old bricks remains visible, marking the start/finish line.

The first NASCAR race was won by local hero Jeff Gordon who was cheered on by a crowd of 350,000, the largest crowd ever to watch a Winston Cup race. Other drivers to have held the much-desired NASCAR's "Brickyard 400" cup aloft are Dale Jarrett, Dale Earnhardt and Ricky Rudd.

Even the fastest stock cars are slower than the monsters that compete in the Indy 500, but as crashes are more common in stock car racing, the outer and inner crash walls were widened to contain the cars in case of an accident. Another noticeable change was that the circuit's famous scoreboard tower had to be made larger to accommodate a Winston Cup's 40 competitors – seven more than Indy car.

The track at Indiana is not steeply banked but is among the fastest tracks in the world. This is because of the added straights between turns one and two and turns three and four.

When crashes happen in NASCAR racing, they can be spectacular.

STAT FILE

Indianapolis Trackfacts

Length	4 km (2.5 miles) oval
Banking	12 degrees on turns

FACT FILE

Qualifying Records	Driver	Speed	Date
WINSTON CUP	B. Bodine	291.916 km/h (181.072 mph)	4.8.00

Race Records	Driver	Speed	Date
WINSTON CUP	B. Labonte	250.916 km/h (155.912 mph)	5.8.00

The old speedsters of the 1920s were usually Ford Model As with factory body parts, but modified engines and chassis – and Ford has been at the heart of stock car racing ever since.

A glance through the history books reveals models such as Tom Young's 1938 Ford Coupe for which he paid $3 (but he found $8 under the floor mat, so he came out ahead), Chris Turner and his "Purple Hog", the Holman and Moody Galaxies of the 1960s, the Torino Talladegas of the 1960s and 70s, and now the Thunderbird.

The current Thunderbirds in which knights of the sport such as Dale Jarrett, Ernie Irvan and Mark Martin compete are among the sleekest stock cars built. Countless hours on the drawing board and in the wind-tunnel test track have produced a car with smooth, rounded edges, a perfectly angled windscreen and sloping roof line that slips smoothly around the circuit.

Ford's engine, restricted in competition by NASCAR rules to 550 hp, can produce up to 750 hp.

Ford had no Winston Cup Champions after 1992 when Alan Kulwicki took the crown, but with top-class drivers and a car of the calibre of the current Thunderbird, experts agreed it could only be a matter of time until they won. In 1999 Dale Jarrett duly obliged.

STAT FILE

FORD THUNDERBIRD

Wheelbase	279.5 cm (110 in)
Weight	1542 kg (3400 lb)
Brakes	Ventilated disc brakes
Engine	5867 cc (358 ci), ohv.1-4V, V8, 700 hp
Transmission	Borg Warner Super T-10, floor-shift, four-speed manual

If you are keen on NASCAR or stock car racing generally, here are some names and numbers that might be useful.

AUSTRALIA
New South Wales Hot Rod Association
PO Box 3068,
Liverpool,
NSW 2170

Victoria Hot Rod Association
PO Box 34,
Oakleigh,
Victoria 3166
Email: ray32@one.net.au

CANADA
Canadian Stock Car Auto Racing
Association (CASCAR),
9763 Gledon Drive,
Komoka
ONT MOL 1RO
Tel: 519-641-1214
Fax: 519-641-1217
Email: racing@cascar.ca
Website: www.cascar.ca

UK
British Stock Car Racing Association
(BRITSCAR) Formula 1,
1 Bellingham,
Wentworth Park,
Wilmcote,
Tamworth,
Staffs
B77 4PE
Tel: 01827 892934
Fax: 01827 897065

British Stock Car Racing Association
(BRITSCAR) Formula 2,
Alan Bunter,
3 PO Buildings,
Templecombe,
Somerset
BA8 0JB
Tel: 01963 370296
Email: alan@bunterbuilt.freeserve.co.uk

USA
American Motor Racing Association
334 North 10th Street,
Coshocton,
Ohio 43812
Tel: 00 1 740 622 7316
Email: doneverhart@hotmail.com
Website: www.amramodified.com

Busch All-Star Series
NASCAR,
PO Box 2875,
Daytona Beach,
Florida 32120
Tel: 904-253-0611
Fax: 904-252-8804
Email: publicrelations@nascar.com
Website: www.nascar.com

International Motor Contest
Association (IMCA)
PO Box 921,
Vinton,
IA 52349
Tel: 319-472-2201
Fax: 319-472-2218
Email: raceimca@aol.com
Website: www.imca.com

NASCAR,
PO Box 2875,
Daytona Beach,
Florida 32120
Tel: 904-253-0611
Fax: 904-252-8804
Email: publicrelations@nascar.com
Website: www.nascar.com

TECHNICAL TERMS

There are some words in this book which you may not have seen before. Here is an explanation of them.

Backstretch: the straight length of a racetrack farthest from the finishing line.

Brakes: the part of a car that makes it slow or stop.

Banking: the angle at which the outer edge of a track rakes upward.

CC: short for cubic centimetres, the measure of an engine's size.

Carburettor: a device that controls the mixing of petrol and air in an engine.

Cockpit: the driving compartment of a racing car.

Engine: a machine inside a car that turns the wheels.

Fuel: normally, petrol or diesel that burns inside a car's engine.

Frontstretch: the long straight section of a race track where drivers cross the finishing line.

Gears: the device that allows the driver to control the speed at which the engine is working.

Horsepower: a measure of an engine's power. The greater the horsepower, the faster the car.

Pits: an area at the side of a race track where cars go to be refuelled, have their tyres changed and be repaired.

Pole position: the best position at the start of a race.

RPM: revs per minute – the rate at which an engine works.

Shock absorbers: part of a car's suspension system.

Sponsorship: money given to a racing team by a company that wants to gain publicity from the team's success.

Timed trials: speed tests where cars are timed over a specified distance.

Track: a surfaced circuit over which cars are raced.

Transmission: a motor car's gearing system.

Tyres: rubber rings filled with air that surround the wheels. Tyres absorb some of the bumps on the track, but more importantly, help the car grip the track.

Wheelbase: the distance between the front and rear axles of a motor car.

INDEX